BOOK OF ART NOUVEAU ALPHABETS & ORNAMENTS

GRAPHIC
ARTS
ARCHIVES
GAA

BOOK OF ART NOUVEAU ALPHABETS & ORNAMENTS

A Sterling/Main Street Book
Sterling Publishing Co., Inc.   New York

For Virginia and Richard

Library of Congress Cataloging-in-Publication Data

Book of art nouveau alphabets & ornaments / Graphic Arts Archives.
     p. cm.
  "A Sterling/Main Street book."
  1. Alphabets. 2. Decoration and ornament—Art nouveau.
I. Graphic Arts Archives.
NK3625.A73B65 1990   90-39132
745.6'197'09034—dc20   CIP

10 9 8 7 6 5 4 3 2 1

A Sterling/Main Street Book

Published 1990 by Sterling Publishing Company, Inc.
387 Park Avenue South, New York, N.Y. 10016
Originally published by Universe Books as
A Book of Art Nouveau Alphabets & Ornamental Designs
Foreword © 1977 by The Main Street Press
Distributed in Canada by Sterling Publishing
℅ Canadian Manda Group, P.O. Box 920, Station U
Toronto, Ontario, Canada M8Z 5P9
Distributed in Great Britain and Europe by Cassell PLC
Villiers House, 41/47 Strand, London WC2N 5JE, England
Distributed in Australia by Capricorn Ltd.
P.O. Box 665, Lane Cove, NSW 2066
Manufactured in the United States of America
All rights reserved

ISBN 0-8069-7427-3

Foreword

Amidst the confusion of Victorian styles that marked the late nineteenth century, one style alone emerged that dared call itself "modern." *Le Style Moderne* spread across Europe in the '80s and '90s, a harbinger of the dynamic and commercial century to come, and took on a variety of names: *Jugendstil, Style Nouille, Style Mêtro, Sezessionsstil, Stile Liberty, Modernismo,* and *Le Style Anglais. Art Nouveau,* as we prefer to call it today, was a resurgence of an essentially decorative, romantic, baroque style that aimed at exploiting the ornamental value of the curved line. The hallmark of full-blown Art Nouveau, consequently, was a sinuous and interlacing line, derived from natural, usually floral, forms, reduced to representational symbols. Although it was in many respects a product more of fashion than of true art, Art Nouveau ultimately influenced the course of modern painting and architecture, the later work of the artists Van Gogh, Seurat, and Toulouse-Lautrec, and the architect Victor Horta, for example, directly influencing the early work of Munch, Kokoshka, and Frank Lloyd Wright. But above all, Art Nouveau was a particularly important element in the revival of such decorative arts as glassware, textiles, bookbinding, posters, and graphic design.

Essentially a European style, Art Nouveau was popularized in turn-of-the-century America through its employment in the designs of the so-called "useful arts" —ceramics, glassware, ironwork, and hardware. The studio of Louis Comfort Tiffany, for example, with its "Favrile" glassware, and Yale & Towne, with its Art Nouveau hardware, were both important in bringing the style to the attention of the American public. But its greatest reflection, and one almost totally ignored today, was its primacy in advertising art.

The period in which Art Nouveau flourished is coincidentally the period in which there developed an entirely new media of American advertising, including bus and car cards, posters, billboards, and direct-mail solicitation. Street-car advertising came into general use about 1890, when the change was made from horse-drawn to electric cars. The mail order field developed rapidly, taking its lead from the introduction of Rural Free Delivery by the federal government in 1896 and from such catalogue houses as Sears, Roebuck and Montgomery Ward, both of which, significantly, employed Art Nouveau lettering to great effect. This was the day, too, of the corner drugstore, with its advertisements in gold leaf on mirrored glass and the ubiquitous, sinuous lettering of the Coca-Cola trademark, still the best known example of Art Nouveau design in the world.

The rise of advertising gave a new opportunity to commercial artists in general and to the designers of alphabets in particular, for it was to be expected that America, the home of advertising, would take full advantage of the vogue for Art Nouveau. Even the most superficial examination of turn-of-the-century advertising reveals a profusion of Art Nouveau alphabets, both in type and in hand-lettering, many of true artistic merit. So prolific, in fact, were these variations on *Le Style Moderne* that, by the beginning of the present century, fashion in lettering proved almost as cyclical as that in women's dress.

"New styles in lettering are created in order that attractive variety may be added to the world of commerce." So wrote an Arrow-collared advertising executive in the opening years of this century. "To be progressive, the advertiser must always use new alphabets before they become ancient history. It is the novelty that makes new faces valuable. They catch the eye of the reader by a change in form and tone of advertising matter. The alphabet that has become the property of all in general loses somewhat its original attraction. Advertisers want the pulling power that goes with novelty—a power to utilize new designs while they are new and stylish. Style in lettering is as valuable as style in literature."

The commercial world took up the use of new designs in lettering with the same alacrity with which it welcomed the telephone as a substitute for the messenger boy, and for the same reasons—better results and more profits. And among the first American commercial artists to realize the value of better results and more profits from the design of stylish and novel alphabets and layouts was a Chicago sign painter named Frank H. Atkinson. His popular manual, *Sign Painting,* first published in 1908, took full advantage of the sinuous, tendril-like forms of Art Nouveau graphics and applied them to the dollar-and-cents world of commercial advertising.

Atkinson believed—correctly so—that lettering is an art. Lettering can create almost any desired impression, express an idea, and even lend distinction to the advertising page or commercial sign. It can suggest quality, charm, action, speed, beauty, dignity, and character. "Hand lettering," he wrote, "can be made to fit awkward shapes and spaces where typography cannot be used. It should carry the message to the reader in the simplest and most pleasing manner." In one sense, advertising art has not changed much in almost three-quarters of a century. In their unending search for "the simplest and most pleasing manner," artists are continually discovering "new" old forms for inspiration, much as Atkinson himself adapted classic alphabets and created them anew as Art Nouveau. His designs for advertising panels and ends, his layouts for Art Nouveau advertisements, and his seventy-five original alphabets were in their time definitive. "No book extant," he claimed, "contains as many alphabets." They are now part of that happy domain called "public" and may be copied freely and frequently without begging anyone's permission. Atkinson's alphabets and layouts have been printed on a paper suitable for purposes of reproduction.

Alphabets

ATKINSON FANCY ROMAN

J. Q. PLOW
MIGHT
VEX Z. D.
BURKE'S
&FANCY&
even job, foxy
bu kin, cuts logs
sqare with an
adz r i i i i 12345
m 8 6 7 1 1 9

R SE F L J K M V W
H D T U A B C D
E F G H I J L M
N O P Q R S T
A B U V W X Y Z
& 1 2 3 4 5 6 7 8 9
a b c d e f g h i j k m l n
R opqrstu R *Alternative*
& vwxyz R R *Alt.*

Modern "1908" Classic

ABCDEFGHIJK
LMNOPQRST
UVWXY Z &

ssabcdefghijk
lmnprtuw

Classic Block

ABCDEFGHIJKLMNO
PQRSTUVWXYZ&
abcdefghijklmnopqr
stuvwxyz

ABCDEFGHIJKL
MNOPQRSTU
VWXYZ&
abcdefghijkl
mnopqrstuvw
xyz123456789
HALF·CLASSIC·ROMAN·

ABCDEFGHIJ
KLMNOPQR
STUVWXY
12345678
Z90&abcdefgh
CHICAGO TUSCAN
ijklmnoprstuv
wxyz

ABCDEFGHIJK
LMNOPQRSTU
VWXY Z&&
abcdefghijkl
mnopqrstuvw
xyz123456789

Modernized Ideal Classic

ABCDEFGHIJ
KLMNOPQR
STUVWXYZ
abcdefghijklmnop
qrstuvwg
8965C&2347

"Bulletin Stub"

A B C D E F G H I
J K L M N O P Q R S
U V W X Y Z

abcdefghijlmnop
qrrrstuvwxyzk

FRENCH ROMAN

ACDBEF
GHIJKL
MNOPORST
UVWXYZ&
123456
7890
adcbefg
hijlmnokprst
quvwxyz

Heavy Sign Script

ABCDEFGH
IJKLMNOQ
PRSUVWXYZ

abcdefghijklmn
soprrrtuvwxyz

Eccentric French

ABCCCDEFFG
JHIKLMNQPRS
TUVWXYZ&

acbdefgͭhijkmnopr
stuvwxyz SS E E
SS &&& SE
E̶

French Roman in General

also Some Modified Alternatives

EE

E NAMES

A
G B C C
a
dcb
DEF
efg
GHIJK
hijlmnok
LMNOPQR
qrstp
STUV
uv
WXY
xwy
Z
z
&

1
423
56789
0

"Spike Spur" French

ABCDEFGH
IJKLMNOP
QRSTUVW
XYZ &
abcdefghijklm
nopqrstuv
wxyz
1234567890

Show Card French

ABCDEFGHI
JKLMNOP
QRSTUVW
XYZ&

aabcdefghijklm
nopqrxystuvwz

aadʃgsw

13245
6789₃

Sign Painters' Plymouth

ABCDEF
GHIJKLMNO
PQRSTUVW
&XYZ&
abcdefghijk
lmnopqrsutvw
xyz
123456
7890

BULLETIN ROMAN.

ABCDEFG
HIJKLMN
OPQRSTUV
WXYZ
abcdefg &
hijklmnopqr
stuwxyz
123456789

ABBCEFGHIDKLMNO
PQRSTUVWXYZabcdefg
hijklmnopqrstuvwxyz &

ABCDEFGHIDKLMNOPQRSTUV
WXYZ RRRPGS
9 aabcdefghijklmnopqrstuvywxyz
& & 12345678

ABCDEFGHIJK
LMNOPQRST
UVWXYZ
abcdefghijklmnopqrs
tuvwxyz &

"CHICAGO" TUSCAN ROMAN

ABCDEFGHIJK
LMNOPQRSTU
VWXYZ&12345
6789abcdefgh
ijklmnopqrstu
vxwzy

MODIFIED TUSCAN ROMAN

ABCDEFGHIJKL
MNOPQRSTUVW
XYZ&12 3456789
abcdefghijklmnopqr
stuvwxyz

ALTERNATIVES CEFGJS
EES FT
EE ALTERNATIVES

·Extreme French

ABCDFGH
IJKLMNOPQ
RSTUV
WXYZ & E

12 34 567 89

abcdefgfhisklm
noopqrsstuv
a wyxz

Modified Antique Tuscan Roman.

ABCDEFGH
IJKLMNOPQ
RSTUVWXY
Z & &
123 45 678 90
pack my box with fve
dozen liquor jugs.

"Single Stroke Tuscan"

GO! LAZY FAT VIX
EN BE SHREWD
JUMP QUICK
pack my box with five dozen
liquor jugs 1234567890

TT Alternate.

Condensed French

ABCDEFGHIJKLM
NOPQRSTUVWXYZ
&12345678
abcdefghijklmnopqrstuvwxyyz
RR

Eccentric French

AABCDEFEFGHIJ
KLMNOPQRSTU
VWXYZ&&

Antique Roman·

ABCDEF
GHIJKLMN
OPQRST
UVWXYZ&
ES Limit of Elongation
abcdefghijklmn
opqrstuvwxyz
123456789

ABCDEF
GHIJKLM
NOPQRS
TUVWXY
Z & & abcd
efghijklmn
o pqrstu v
wxyz 1234
567890.

"Stonehouse"Egyptian.

ABCDEFGHIJKLMNQPRR STUVWXYZ&

abcdefghijklmnopqrstuvwxyz

Engrossing Text

ABCDEFEFGHIJK LMNOPQRSTVU WXYZ

abcdefghijklmnopqrstuvvxyz

abcdefghijklmnopqrrstuvvxyz

Heavy Egyptian

ABCDEFGHIJ
KLMNYQPR
STUVWXZ&

Antique Thick & Thin

ABCDEFGHIJKL
MNOPQRSTU
VWXYZ&

·Egyptian·

ABCDEFGHIJK
LMNOPRSTU
VWXYZ & 12

x   345678   y

cefghijkn9mopqrstu
abzvw

Sign Painters' De Vinne.

ABCDEFGH
IJKLMNOPQ
RSTUVWX
YZ & & &
1234567890
abcdefghmnopqr
uvwstxyz

GO!
LAZY FAT
VIXEN
BE SHREWD;
JUMP
QUICK!

abcd & efghi

jkmlnop

qrstuvwyz

198234567

TUSCAN BLOCK (heavy.)

"ADVERTISERS" "THICK & THIN PLUG"

A
B C
D E F
G H I J K
L M N O P Q R
S T U V
W X Y
Z &

a d c b e f g h i j l m n
o k q r s t p u v w x y z
1 4 5 7 8
2 3 6 9

AaBbCcDdEeFfGg
HhIiJjKkLlMmNnOo
PpQqRrSsTtUuVv
WwXxYyZz 123459876

ABCDEFGHIJKLMN
OPQRSTUVWXYZ
12345 & 6789
abcdefghijklm
nopqrstuvwxyz

GUNNING "SINGLE STROKE"

WESTERN "LIGHT" TUSCAN ROUND BLOCK

A B C D E F
G H I J K
L M N O
P Q R
S T
U
V W
X Y Z
&

Tuscan Full Block

ABCDEFGH
IJKLOMNP
QRSTUVWX
12YZ&abcde34
fgghijkkl&m
567npqrtuy890

Full Block (Thick & Thin)

ABCDEFGHI
JKLMNOPQ
RSTUVWYZ&
abcdefghijklmn
opqrtuvwyyz
12 2 345678 90

Broken Poster

ABCDEFGH
IJKLMNOP
QRTUVWX
YZ&

abcdefghijkl
mnopqrstuv
wxyz
123456789

ROUND BLOCK (Thick&Thin)

ABCDE
FGHIJK
LMNOPQ
RSTUVW
XYZ&ab
cdefghij
klmnop
qrstu
vwyz
123456789

Poster Block No2.

ABCCDDEF
NNOPPQR
GHIJJKLM
RTSSUVWX
YZ&

abcdefghijlcmnl
opqrstuvwxyz

"1908" Classic "Plug"

ABCDEFGHIJKLMN
OPQRSTUVWXYZ&

abcdefgghijklmnopq
rstuvwxyz

ABCDEF GHI
JKLMNO PQ
RSTUVWXY
Z&

stuvwxyyz
S ab cd
efghijklmnopqr
"?;:1234567890

Limit of Elongation

ABCDEF GHIJKLMN
OPQRSTU VWXYZ&
aabcdefghijklmnopqr
stuvwxyz123456 7
890 C S

Spur Egyptian

ABCDEFGHIJ
KLMNOPQRS
TUVWXYZ&

Modifications (Light)

ÆBCSG
ABCSJG·CSJG·CSG·
JQSCSFM
123456789 Ss

Spur Egyptian

ABCCDFEGGHJJKL^L
MNOPQRSSTUVW
XYZ&

abcdefghijklmnn
opqrstuvwxyz

Spur Egyptian (Light)

ABCDEFGHJKLMNOPQRS
TUVWXYZ&

abcdefghijklmnopqrstuvwxyz
123456789

·Antique Block·

A B C D E F G
H I J K L M N O
P Q R S T U V
W X Y Z a b c d e f
g h i j k l m n o p q r
s t u v w x y z 1 2
3 4 5 6 7 8 9 & &

A B C C C G D E F G H I J
K L M N O P Q R R R S S T
U V W X Y Z a b c d e f g h i j k
l m n o p q r s t u v w x y z
&1 2 2 3 3 4 5 6 7 8 9

·Single Stroke·Block·

·Single Stroke·Block·

ABCDEFGHIJKLMNXOPQRSS
TUVVWYZ abcdefghijkhhnprlmmnno
pqrstuvwxyz 1234567890

AaaaBbcdeEfFGhhijklmnopqrstu
uvwwxyz

ABCDEFGHIJKLMNOPQREFC
GSUTVWXYZabcdefghijklmn
opqrstuvwxyz ABCDEFGHIJKLMNOPQRSTUVWXYZ
abcdefghijklmnopqrstuvwxyz
abcdefghijklmnopqrstuvwxwz

ABC DEFGHIJJ KLMNOPQRR SST
UVWXYZ&

Round Full Block

ABCDEFH
GIJKLMNO
PQRSTUV
WXYZ&abc
defghijklmnopq
rstuvwxyyz 123
4567890

Fancy Roman.

ABCDEFG
HIJKLMN
OPQRSTU
VWXY&
Z II

Bulletin 'Plug'

ABCDEFGHIJK
LMNOPQRTUV
WXYZ&
abcdefghijklm
nopqrstuvwxyz

Fancy Roman / Bulletin Plug   54

POSTER BLOCK

ABCDEFGH
IJKLMNOP
QRSTUVW
XYZ&

abcdefghijkmnopq
rstuvwxyz

2345678910

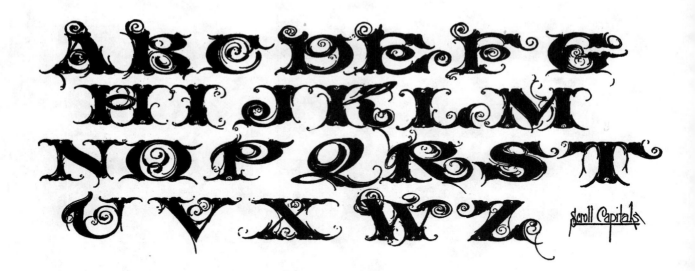

ABCDEFGHIJ
KLMNOP
QRSTUVWX
YZ & French Plug RRS

Art Nouveau

ABCDEFE
GHIJKL
MNOPQRS
TUWXYZ

ABCDEFGHI
JKLMNOPQRS
TUWXYZ Eccentric Roman

Art Nouveau / Eccentric Roman   58

BRADLEY

ЯABCDEFGH
IJKLOMNPQ
RSTUVWX
X & YZ & K

aabbcddeefghki
jklmnnoppqr
rsstuuvvwxy
rz

A
BC
DEF
GHIJK
LMNOPQR
STUV
WXY
Z&

FRENCH ROMAN (LIGHT)

4123
956
78
O

a
dcb
efg
hijlmnok

pstq
uvw
xy
z

A B C D E
F G H I J K
L M O P Q
R S T U V
W X Y Z
&

ABCDEFGGGHIJKLMNO
PPPRRRSTUWVXYZ&
aabcdefgghijklmn
opqrstuvwxyz
123456789

Modified "Plug"

ABCDEFGHJK
LMNQPRSTSSU
VWXYZ & 12345
6789 EFF abcdefgh
ijklmnoprstuvwxyz

A
B C
R DEF R
GHIJK
LMNOPQR
STUVWXYZ
& (heavy) FRENCH ROMAN

24567 RR
319 a
8 dcb sp
efg
hijlmnok
qstpuvw
xyz

B C lmn O
P F N L
R T M I
V G S Z
H U S O
Y U abc X
K z W
uvw A
xyz hijk defg
rst opq

Layouts

Panels
&
Ends

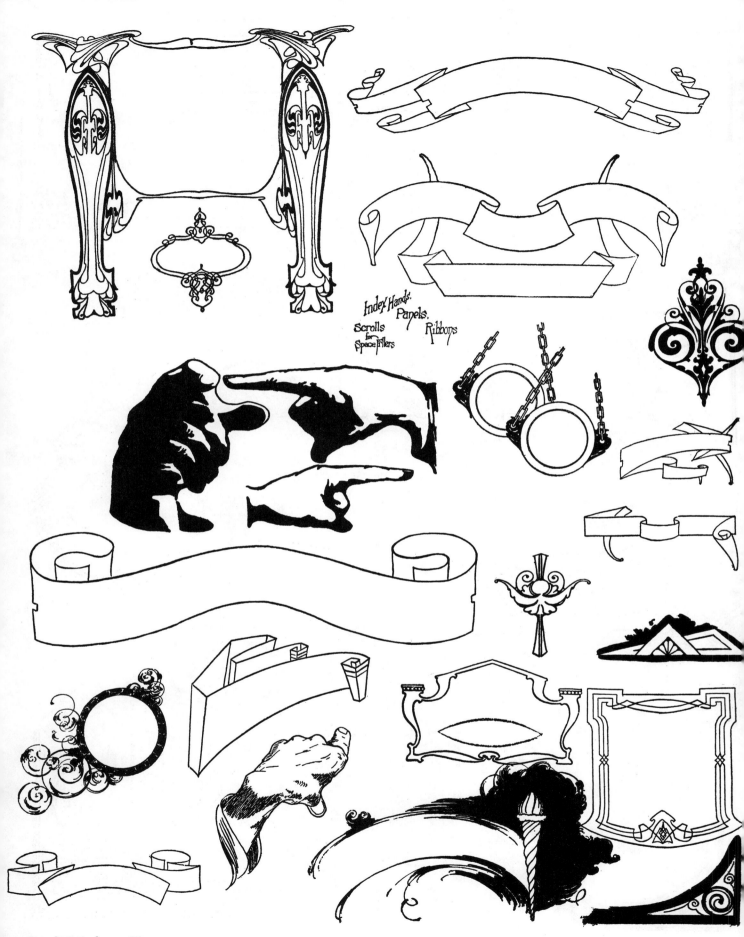

Index Hands.
Panels.
Scrolls
for
Space Fillers
Ribbons

Panels.
Corner Pieces.
Scrolls
for
"Panel
Ends"

SIGNS

·I·B· PERRY ·CO·

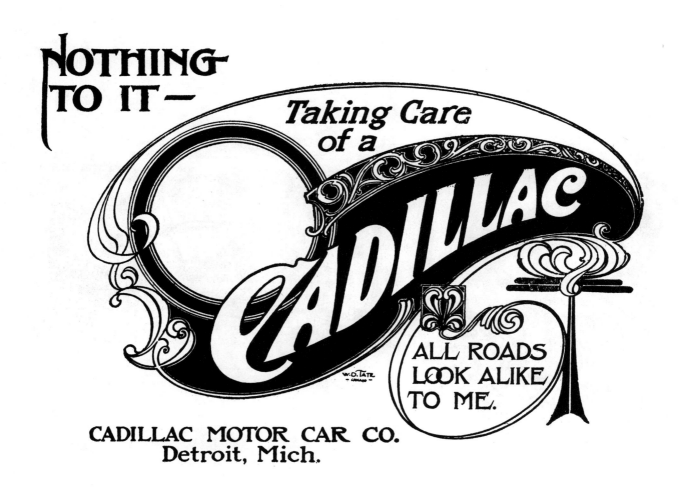

ALL ROADS LOOK ALIKE TO ME.

CADILLAC MOTOR CAR CO.
Detroit, Mich.

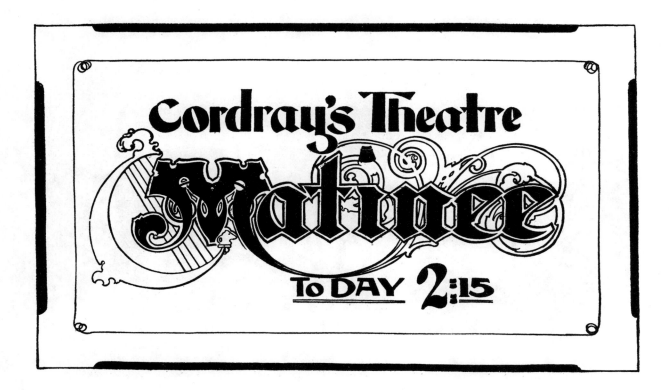

A·R·HUSSEY
Designer   Manfrer
SIGNS

HEADQUARTERS FOR TOYS FOR XMAS IMPORTED NOVELTIES.

H·C· BODER, SIGN PAINTER

PHONE SO-512.

80

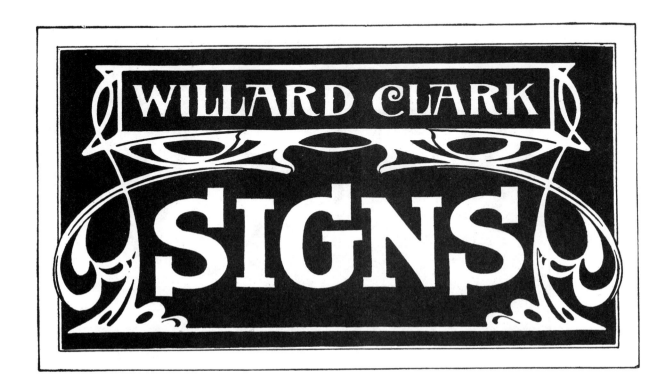

46

UP TO DATE

SIGNS

Abbott
AND
·CO·

CLASSIC
AND
ARTISTIC
MODERNISMS.

PHONE ·SQ·1058·

Manhattan Theatre

A·H·
WOODHULL
Manager

After Extensive Alterations
This House will open early in September
Presenting only High Class Plays.

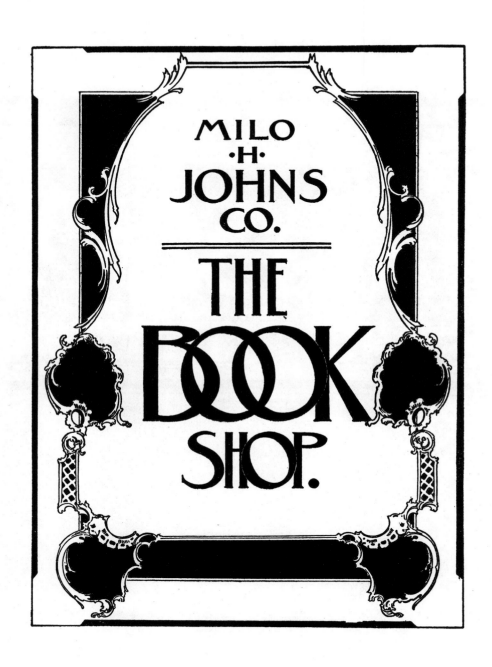

THE
MILLINERY
IMPORTING
CO.

RESTAURANT

FOR
LADIES
AND GENTLEMEN.

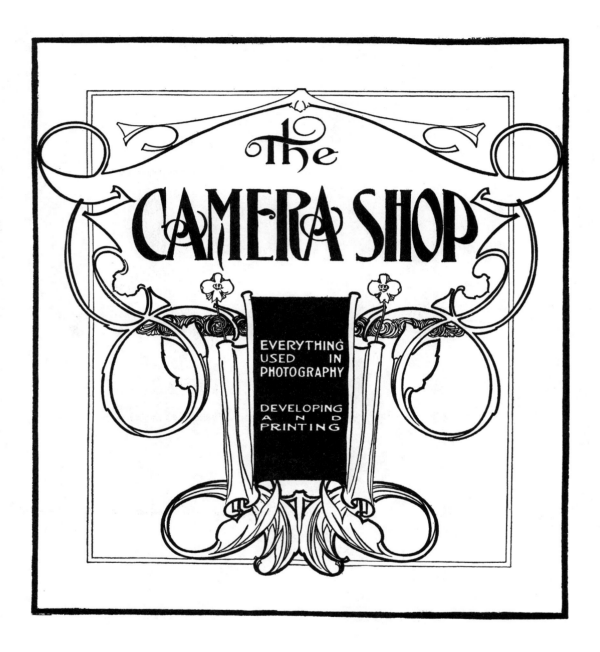

The Camera Shop

EVERYTHING USED IN PHOTOGRAPHY

DEVELOPING AND PRINTING

ART
DEPARTMENT
MAIN FLOOR ·· CENTRE ISLE

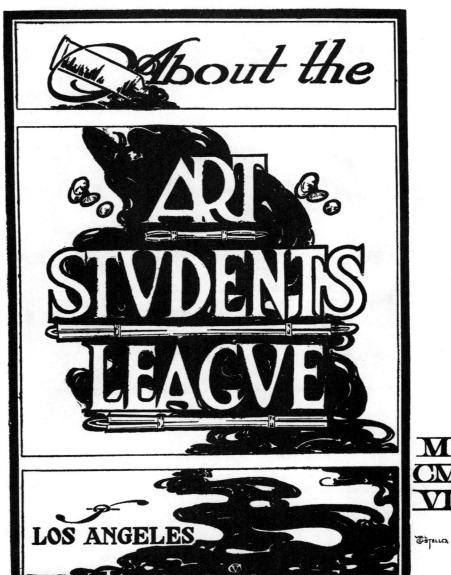

About the

ART
STVDENTS
LEAGVE

LOS ANGELES

MCMVI

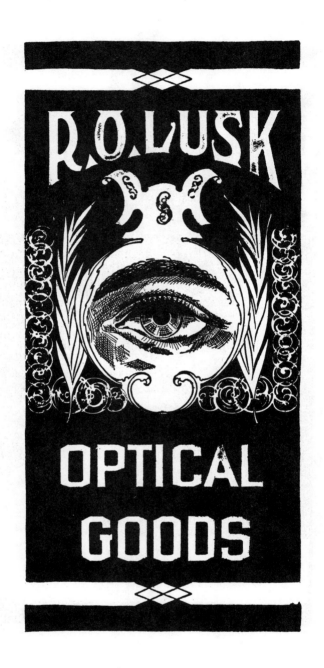

Chicago Academy of Fine Arts

8 E. Madison   8th Floor.

The Directors request the honor of
your company at the Annual Exhibition
of Charcoal Drawings done by the
Students of the night class under
W. J. Reynolds.

March 8th to 29th.

ROOKWOOD POTTERY

Highest award
at nine expositions

Marshall field
& Company

Rookwood Room
Third floor
Annex.

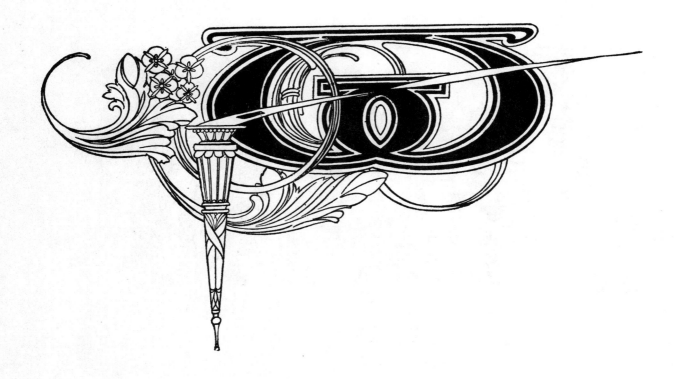